MW01139901

Pain &

Renewal:

A Poetry Anthology

Compiled and Edited
by Vita Brevis Press

Contents

Introduction 1

PAIN 3

    Under the Japanese Cherry Tree - Naida Mujkić 5

    It's About the Bees - J.A. Carter-Winward 6

    Saudade II – John Jeffire 8

    Heading North Are Two Highways – Barrett Warner 10

    Together Apart - Carole Cohen 12

    The Flag of Pain - Gabriela M. 14

    Temple – Katy Santiff 15

    Fatuity - Les Epstein 16

    Storage - Kevin J. McDaniel 18

    Twins – Barrett Warner 20

    Reading – Thomas M. McDade 21

    Domestic Noose – Pauline May 22

    Of Light and Love - J. Lynn Lunsford 24

    Suspending – Gordon Shields 26

    A Man Gets Up on Stage - James Cole 27

    A Late Goodbye - Frances Daggar Roberts 29

    Crossroad - Marilyn Humbert 30

    The Abandoned Dawn – M. Taggart 32

    God is an Earthquake – Harold Strauss 33

    Kintsugi – Merril D. Smith 35

    Another Storm – Phillip Knight Scott 36

    Drops - Stacey Z Lawrence 38

In Memory of My Father - Shalini Pattabiraman 40

Demensch - Jean Fineberg 42

Protection - Judith Capurso 44

Water Levels - Alex Dreppec 45

My Mother's Secret - Linda Imbler 47

Forgotten - Shalini Pattabiraman 48

End of Year Review - Kelly Jayne McCann 51

Rip Tide Ride - Pauline May 52

Patterns - Steve May 54

Washup row - Matt McGee 56

industrial garden - J.A. Carter-Winward 58

Pre-Op - John Jeffire 60

The Baltimore Batechism - Thomas M. McDade 62

Alone - Carson Pytell 64

Bad Weather - Philip Pholeros Porter 65

Liberation - Kelly Jayne McCann 66

Kin Kelli 4: Creed- Katy Santiff 67

Farewell - Suzanne Cottrell 68

Survivor's Guilt - Taylor Ashley King 69

Somewhere in the Mountains - Harold Strauss 71

From One Widow to Another - Erina Booker 72

Autumn Healing - Gabriela M. 73

Soldier - Linda Imbler 74

Grief - Sharon Arthur 76

Videos You've Kept of Me - Jonah Carlson 78

Without Wheels - Sterling Warner 79

Pinking Dock - Stephen Kingsnorth 81

Who's Left to Row the Boat - Ivor Steven 83

Our Pain Won't Go Away - Walt Page 84

Unwound – Ken Gierke 85

RENEWAL 87

Earth is God - Naida Mujkić..89

Cicada – Karla Whitmore 91

Homarus americanus – Shanna Maybright.......................................92

The Amaryllis - Theresa Burns 94

River Man – Harold Strauss 95

Holding Stones - Karen Shepherd 96

Under Leaden Clouds - Jim Brosnan 97

Consider the Lily – William Sterne 98

Picking Up the Sun – Graham Wood...99

The Birth - M. Taggart...100

Kin Kelli 7: Blow – Katy Santiff 102

Pollen Path - Judith Capurso 103

Telogen Winter, 2010 - Oormila Vijayakrishnan Prahlad 104

Revival – Cynthia Pitman..106

Your Heaven - J. Lynn Lunsford..108

My Mother's Voice - Charles Murray 110

The Edge of Time – Ann Christine Tabaka.......................................111

The Seed – Marsha Warren Mittman 113

A Stick – Dan A. Cardoza 114

Riddle of Renewing – J. lewis 115

Encounter with a Kung Fu Master - Karla Whitmore.......................117

Visiting With Chaos – Ali Grimshaw..118

Salvation - Megha Sood 119

Unnoticed - Jim Brosnan..121

Baseball – Carson Pytell 122

The Scribe and the Prophet - Greg Ramkawsky 123

Incubator – Ali Grimshaw 124

Turning Point – Merril D. Smith 125

Little Moth Dancing - Joseph Marshall 126

Thrive - Catherine Zickgraf 128

After Rejection - Theresa Burns 129

Introduction

There are as many forms of pain as there are paths to renewal, and I can think of no better way to explore this than through collected stories of people from around the world. In the same way the broader themes of a good book are not conveyed in one line but through many small and dispersed instances, the broader truths of pain and renewal bare their patterns when the struggles and victories of the individual are placed alongside those of the many. Read from cover to cover, I believe many of these patterns can be found in this anthology.

Putting the anthology together also had its lessons. Given the choice to write about pain or renewal, almost every poet chose pain - often exclusively. It seems that we're much more willing to dissect and dwell on the harder parts of life than those parts that go right. For this reason, rather than balance each section into halves, I let pain take up the majority of this book. If poetry captures the human experience, and that is overwhelmingly defined by a fixation on pain, then let it be represented as such here. If nothing else, it makes renewal that much more profound.

INTRODUCTION

PAIN

"A man pays dearly for being immortal: to this end he must die many times over during his life."

- Friedrich Nietzsche, *Ecce Homo: How One Becomes What One Is*

PAIN

Under the Japanese Cherry Tree - Naida Mujkić

Under the Japanese cherry tree blooming by the road
An old dog died
It was a cross-breed that's been kicked out
And thrown rocks and butts at, anything they came across
It was around three o'clock in the afternoon
I was on my way back from the supermarket
Carrying a shopping bag over my shoulder, he was lying down like dogs do,
But since chicken giblets didn't revive his instinct
I pushed him with the tip of my sandal
Soft gray hairs on which petals were falling
Or something else totally invisible
I'm staring at the cherry tree that doesn't appear worried
I see myself at last, children are passing by me licking ice creams
Ladies with bows in their hair, fathers of favourites.

Because this is the order of things
I stood under the Japanese cherry tree
And waited for my turn calmly

Naida Mujkić, PhD. Her work has appeared in literary journal and anthologies around the world. So far, she published five books of poetry and one book of lyrical prose. She has participated in several international poetry and literature festivals.

It's About the Bees - J.A. Carter-Winward

Turning on the light—
it's night outside and my son—I was
up, waiting. Remembering when I was

too sick to wait. Not hearing him
not come home. Not hearing his absent
breath. I told my husband to come look.

On the porch, I said. The bees, they're
everywhere, there, there, see? Dead. I opened the
front wooden door, the leaded beveled glass

creating colors that weren't there.
What do you think it means, I asked.
It isn't bees, he replied. *It's yellowjackets.*

I remembered then, when my son told me once
they had no purpose. That yellowjackets were not
helpful, they were not food. Yellowjackets

were a scourge on the earth and deserved to
die because they had no purpose. They just
were. Like a burst appendix. Like a sick

mother who showed her son death and
despair in her eyes too soon. Like a son
with pinpoint-pupils and a chalked-skin outline

bordering his gaunt face, his perfect
rusted-penny hair dyed black for no reason
or purpose other than to not be himself.

It means, my husband said, *the bug-spray guys
did their jobs.* He got the broom and swept
their still-twitching bodies off the porch.

And I don't know why that wasn't a
good enough answer for me but it didn't
matter just then because we fixed the

porch light. It's on and the nights are
still warm and my son—he's sure, now to
find his way home.

*J.A. Carter-Winward is an award-winning poet, literary novelist,
playwright, musician, film/visual artist, and performer. Author of 11
books, her work has appeared in the anthology, We Will Be Shelter
(Write Bloody Publishing), HSTQ, Desert Wanderings Literary
Journal, and Vita Brevis. J.A. is also a contributing writer to several
online publications, including Mad in America: Science, Psychiatry
and Social Justice.*

Saudade II - John Jeffire

I started wearing your perfume
Last week after I ran out of
Aftershave, you know, your bottle
With the fancy flower shaped
Glass lid, I don't know the name,
And then I began wearing your pajamas,
The blue ones with the holes I should
Have replaced months ago. And I
Hope you're laughing as you
Read this, because of all my jobs—
Run to the grocery store at midnight
For mango ice cream guy,
I hate to say this because we're
Already in bed but I left my
Cellphone in the car guy, or honey,
The dog shit on the carpet guy—
My favorite job, the one I feel
I'm best at and enjoy most,
Is being your clown. I wasn't
Born a crusted set of pennies
Under the passenger side floor mat,
You just found me that way, camped
In a mattress on the living room carpet,
Two crates for a dining room table,
A blender, plenty of dog food, the
Frig empty except a twelve of IPA,
So what I mean, what I'm trying
To say in some small way, is Lady,
Come home, soon, please come home.

John Jeffire was born in Detroit. His novel Motown Burning was named 2005 Grand Prize Winner in the Mount Arrowsmith Novel Competition and 2007 Gold Medal Winner for Regional Fiction in the Independent Publishing Awards. His first book of poetry, Stone + Fist + Brick + Bone, was a 2009 Michigan Notable Book Award nominee. Former U.S. Poet Laureate Philip Levine called the book "a terrific one for our city." His most recent poetry collection, Shoveling Snow in a Snowstorm, was published by the Finishing Line Press in 2016.

Heading North Are Two Highways
– Barrett Warner

One is meant for anger.
It cleaves New Jersey into knobby halves.
The other is for crying.
At Scranton, it dog legs to the Poconos.

I draft behind a queue of trucks
with Carolina tags, and Illinois, and Maine.
We come from everywhere
and all of us are sobbing.

My mother calls. I blow my nose.
No, I say, I didn't get a haircut.
I didn't remember to shave my chin.
I am so blue I forget to do anything.

Clearer than any sadness,
razors and rumble strips don't jive.
Outside Port Jervis, billboards
advertise truck stop masseurs by the minute.

I park between two idling rigs.
A man, beautiful once,
hip hikes into the large closet
as if he were still curious about love.

I can't take off my clothes fast enough.
He tries not to notice my bloody face.
How much does it hurt, he crows.
It sounds like *Jesus. Jesus. Jesus.*

Barrett Warner is the author of Why Is It So Hard to Kill You? (Somondoco, 2016) and My Friend Ken Harvey (Publishing Genius, 2014). His work appears in Beloit Poetry Journal, Pirene's Fountain, and elsewhere. He lives in South Carolina, in the wild mushroom heaven along the South Edisto River.

Together Apart - Carole Cohen

When dawn strokes the horizon,
I sit chilled, huddled
in my jacket and blanket on the porch,
hands around a hot cup of coffee,
listening to yawns
from the awakening woods.
For five years, in the early morning,
we have started our days together apart,
drinking coffee, talking about our love.
The miles between us are long.
Sadly, we will never see each other again,
but have the lifelines of phone calls,
marveling at how alike we are.
Differences only complement each other.
I will hold up the telephone
so you can hear the owl hooting
at the same time I do.
Shivering in anticipation and cold,
I wait for your call.

When sun trails his orange scarf
over the mountain as he leaves the sky,
I sit on the screened porch as usual
listening to the final conversations of birds,
the owl warming up for his nightly hunt.
I wait for your call so we can reminisce
about when we used to sit across
the table, each writing poetry.
In the small hours of the morning

sit there again eating cobbler and ice cream.
We know we are making new memories
with our telephone calls, like making
love in a different way. When you call,
I will gather in your voice.

The phone rings.

Carole Cohen has been widely published in many literary magazines and anthologies. She was the Senior Poetry Editor for Boulevard Literary Magazine. She spent most of her life in St. Louis, but now lives in Chattanooga, TN.

The Flag of Pain - Gabriela M.

I open doors which you can't see
under my father's heavy eyelids
tenderness gets harder every day
I ache and cry
inside the same sunset in which you left
the smell of morphine saturates my skin
in Campo de' Fiori people still sell grapes
some still believe the Freudian nonsense about sex
gale winds blow the dark flag of pain
a lonely boat sits anchored in the bay
my soul is scattered in the west

a lonely phase which reads
tomorrow is already yesterday

Gabriela M. is a US university professor and author of three novels. Her poetry was published by Spillwords Press, Vita Brevis, Gioielli Rubati Poetry:32, Tuck Magazine, and other journals and newspapers. She was selected "Author of the Month" (April 2019) at Spillwords. Her work was included in the anthology America's Emerging Poets Southeast Region (Z Publishing House, 2018) and Florida's Best Emerging Poets 2019 (Z Publishing House, August 19, 2019). Christina Schwarz, the author of the New York Times Bestseller "Drowning Ruth," on Gabriela's poetry: "With lush language and lavish imagery, Gabriela M. evokes a fantastic world ripe with emotion."

Temple - Katy Santiff

On the day you died, I prayed before round
golden gods, made their bronze bell giant ring
and when the log-like mallet struck its home,
I felt the way old metals sing–that tone
reached through my flesh and wrapped around my bones.
That sound's a phantom press when I'm alone.

Katy Santiff has written poetry in various forms all her life. A fan of meter and rhyme, she loves lines that hypnotize the reader with their sound. She believes in densely packed poems, preferring them to be mouthfuls when read aloud. A lifelong Marylander, she loves waterside living, and currently lives in Annapolis, Maryland. Her works have been published in Vita Brevis, Spillwords Press, and Uppagus Magazine.

Fatuity - Les Epstein

Winter argues for its rank:

For a little ice on a Tuesday—
Appears as expected—
Enough to devour white blossoms
Off the Bradford Pears

Enough to seize branches and leaves
And your face sits in like shock—
Cerulean capsules tight in fingertips—
Your wrecked body warming a handsome kitchen
And considering the swallowing of another's pill

Perhaps the right Coffee
Might hasten your Spirit
Out from under
What Chaucer's brothers and sisters
May have called fatuity—
For I am certain I see within you
A rebellion against this glacial

Dissolve of Memory.
What a ferocious bite you have received.
Shadowing looms over your former pleasantries:
DiMaggio and polemics and spouse...
All fade from your catalogue of concerns

If I were a miner
I'd be trepanning your skull

After memories no longer at the ready
For you
Firmly with white-knuckled hold of the kitchen table

Join bowls of tuna and oranges in still life

You do warm the kitchen—
A father Lear grasping at a decision
Should you devour something other than creamed wheat...
And as evening fades on this wretched diurnal

Only Chenoweth on television remains...

For when she sings
From that 'Miserable' musical
"Bring him home! Bring him home!"
You rise from your shock
And roundly applaud a desperate song sung light

Then as with winter
You struggle for your rank,
Briefly reclaiming your old estate
Forever divided by the enigmatic—
Holding on to Chenoweth's chiming tones:
Should air and circumstance
Suddenly lift you up and away to a finer Lodge.

Les Epstein is a poet, playwright and opera librettist. His work has appeared in journals in the United States, Philippines, India and the U.K. Recent credits include Jelly Bucket, Eyedrum Periodically, Mojave River Review, Fourth & Sycamore and Saudade. Cyberwit recently released a collection of his short plays and libretti (Seven). He teaches in Roanoke, VA.

Storage - Kevin J. McDaniel

Inside Daddy's building
that Mama swears looks like
a hobo's bungalow,

my brother and I dig
through buckets of rust flakes
for Daddy's tools.

After his heart attack,
Mama said, *Let the eyesore go.*
But please, save

your daddy's tools.
Keep them.
My brother wipes wrenches,

ratchets, spark plug pliers.
Under a ratty truck seat,
I find Daddy's drill.

Look here! I cry, pretending
to pop slugs again
like an Eastwood character.

I hear Daddy cuss crooked screws
as he drills the picnic table
where we wolfed potato wedges

after Pop Warner practices.
On this rotting floor, I feel
the frazzled cord.

(First published in the *Anthology of Appalachian Writers*)

Founder and an editor of Speckled Trout Review, Kevin J. McDaniel is the author of two chapbooks and a book of poetry, Rubbernecking (Main Street Rag Publishing, 2019). His poems have appeared in the Anthology of Appalachian Writers, Broad River Review, California Quarterly, Cloudbank, Coal City Review, Free State Review, Green Briar Review, North Dakota Quarterly, Ocean State Review, The Offbeat, Valley Voices: A Literary Review, and others. He lives in Pulaski, Virginia.

Twins – Barrett Warner

The hand without feeling
resembles the hand that feels.

Both have sixty or so small bones
and five stocky fingers.

These hands have been friends
since either can remember.

Now, the good hand feels for both.
The bad hand waves, as if to agree with every word.

One side holds forth, the other hopes
doors will open without knobs.

Falling on a muddy trail last week,
the bad hand broke the crash, cracking bones.

A valley cut across my palm
and two fingers refused to buddy-up.

In spite of its strange new shape,
it was entirely painless.

The good hand never stopped singing, nor once offered
to staunch the widening geranium of blood.

*Barrett Warner is the author of Why Is It So Hard to Kill You?
(Somondoco, 2016) and My Friend Ken Harvey (Publishing
Genius, 2014). His work appears in Beloit Poetry Journal, Pirene's
Fountain, and elsewhere. He lives in South Carolina, in the wild
mushroom heaven along the South Edisto River.*

Reading – Thomas M. McDade

Martin Eden chose suicide
By swimming, leapt off
An Ocean liner,
To quit the race
Edna Pontellier also
Swam to her end
In the Gulf of Mexico
Drowning words and sea
Images surrounded Lily
Bart but O. D. by chloral
Hydrate swept her under
Characters in novels linked
In classrooms, bodysurf
To an old man's feet
His toes curled in sand
Stones and shells
To steady himself
Paging neaps
And ebbs
Of his own

Thomas M. McDade is a 73-year-old resident of Fredericksburg, VA, previously CT and RI. He is a graduate of Fairfield University, Fairfield, CT. McDade is twice a U.S. Navy Veteran serving ashore at the Fleet Anti-Air Warfare Training Center, Virginia Beach, VA and at sea aboard the USS Mullinnix (DD-944) and USS Miller (DE /FF 1091).

Domestic Noose – Pauline May

Hear me in the lies I tell the baby
to get him down for his nap.
Hear me in the hard non stop dripping
of the kitchen cold tap.

Hear me walking on eggshells
across this creaking hell.
Hear me smoothing on foundation
to cover up the welts.

Hear me in the cursing of the dishwater
escaping down the sink.
Hear my self-esteem squelch down,
unroll itself and shrink.

Hear me in my name,
'stupid bitch', 'waste of space'.
Hear me saying sorry
for my silly mistakes.

Hear me in my sigh of relief
when he's gone from the flat,
a solitary echo,
all my friendships smashed.

Hear me in what I don't say
when asked if I'm okay.
Hear me in stock phrases
that don't give myself away.

Hear me in the damson
thunder swell of a bruise.
Hear me in the creak of hope
tomorrow will improve.

Hear my favourite music;
those tender love songs.
Hear me in the silence
when I bite my tongue.

Pauline lives in Sunderland, UK, with her husband and cat. She enjoys performing at spoken word events across the north east of England and further afield. She has had poems published in The Writers Cafe, YorkMix magazine, The Blue Nib, Not Your Mother's Breast Milk, and Orbis. In June she won a Mslexia Mini Max competition judged by Helen Mort.

Of Light and Love - J. Lynn Lunsford

The last man to walk on the moon
Once told me what it was like to speed
Through the blackness between
Here and there.

The thing, he said, is that
There actually is no darkness in space.
The Universe is filled with Light,
Some of it older than comprehension.

It travels in invisible silence
Until one day it illuminates us.
It lights our journey,
And reveals us for who we really are.

That's the way it is with Love,
Particularly when forged in a heart
As pure and fierce
As the furnace of a star.

Love sustains us long after the source is gone.
Once created, it voyages unimpeded
Across the vastness,
Lighting the places where memories live.

J. Lynn Lunsford is a Fort Worth, Texas, writer. He works as a communications manager for the Federal Aviation Administration. Before joining the FAA in June 2009, Lunsford was aerospace editor for The Wall Street Journal. He was a member of a team of reporters whose work earned the Journal the 2001 Pulitzer Prize for Breaking News Reporting for coverage of the Sept. 11 attacks on the World Trade Center and the Pentagon. He writes poetry on an antique typewriter when nobody is looking.

Suspending – Gordon Shields

These branches spread like wings over the water's edge
They slowly droop and dip into the shore below
The eroded roots will show through, exposed to those who look
between the mossy rocks
Frozen trees with frosted tops, in wintertime they fall
But for each ancient pine that drops, a new one springs to life
And summer brings the summer sun to watch the saplings stretch
and flap their wings
The outstretched limbs again will droop and dip and drop and fall
To the rhythm of decay

Gordon Shields is a recent graduate of the English Literature and Rhetoric program at the University of Waterloo in Ontario, Canada. Gordon currently tutors ESL students while working to complete his Master's in Political Science. He is a marathon runner, boxer, rock climber, and boggle enthusiast.

A Man Gets Up on Stage - James Cole

Elected but best only in show
not substance
> (of course not substance)
> Because the content
> that is him, isn't all his
> Is this the way we become
> obscured in our own
> poorly scribbled signature?
> Our hands so quick
> to sign away that we forget
> to sign at all?

Did you know that you can command
an army sprung from your own body?
You need only to dial back the degrees
or find a deeper cold, like terror
and soon you'll have two thousand
little soldier's standing on end
all you and yet each
{expendable}

I learned this, but remained impotent
insular and—no this is not the part where you
tell me all my virtues through the shrinking
crack in the door
Perhaps I was too concerned
with satisfaction to be satisfied

Wash your face of me
sleep in
I'm sure that when the time comes
you can quote my silence
for the audience
and some of them will pretend
to have met me on a bus
a long way lost in the rain

James Cole is a graduate student at the University of Virginia. His work has appeared in the The Gallery, Winged Nation, and Virginia Bards Anthology. His forthcoming chapbook, "Crow, come home," will be released in the autumn of 2019 by VerbalEyze Press.

A Late Goodbye - Frances Daggar Roberts

Standing here
in the night of your loss
I am transfixed by the sound of your voice
holding me apart from the reality of death.
While I was still in Europe
you left a message on my landline
from your hospital bed.

Three days later I had returned
to be greeted by your sweet low English tones.
Though the form of you was emptied
the thief of futures could not take your voice from me.
There it was repeating softly
Frances darling I think it's nearly time
that you were home...

Again and again I play the call
a rift in time where you are captured
exactly as you always were.

Frances Daggar Roberts is an Australian poet whose love of plants, animals, landscape and music, permeates much of her writing. Frances is also a psychologist whose work with people who struggle with intense anxiety and depression has added a particular insight and sensitivity to her writing about those who face loneliness and loss.

Crossroad - Marilyn Humbert

soon she will hear
boots beside the bed
scraping bare-boards
the thud, thud, his fists
breaking this morning's promise

a full moon lingers
in greyness before dawn
this time her own
when salt-laden wind
carries a new day's hope

her path is steep
close to the cliff edge
where monstrous shale blocks
cleaved from raw knuckled rock
shatter the surf below

and birds sweep
eddy in formation
above woodlands
following blind curves
on the trail's other side

in the shadow
of the sheer-face
the forest whispers
... she watches gulls in flight

Marilyn Humbert lives in the Northern suburbs of Sydney NSW Australia. Her tanka and haiku appear in international and Australian journals, anthologies and online. Her free verse poems have been awarded prizes in competitions and some have been published.

The Abandoned Dawn – M. Taggart

He wished the door wouldn't again open;
knowing he'd be forced to become another
version of himself. Placed unto him from a
variation of life not meant to be seen, or felt,
or lived. Now- the footsteps, so very light,
unheard by the household so late at night,
but felt by the boy, each and every vibration,
knowing it would be soon time to close his
eyes and beckon the rising moon to please take
him along with its translucent majesty high
above where his being felt the covers being lifted.

Matt is a loving father and husband. Matt has been published in America's Emerging Literary Fiction Writers: Northeast Regions, 2019 (Z Publishing House), America's Emerging Horror Writers: East Region, 2019 (Z Publishing House), Massachusetts's Emerging Writers; An Anthology of Fiction, 2018 (Z Publishing House), Vita Brevis Press, The Drabble, proletaria, and was nominated author of the month of June, 2018, on Spillwords Press.

God is an Earthquake - Harold Strauss

The seeing have forgotten
That the world persists when they
Turn a corner or shut their eyes,

That the young woman they met
The other day was not conjured into being
By her falling in their glance
Any more than she was snuffed
Out of life by her falling out;

That the human drama in the marrow
Of the soul is not resolved by
Busying the mind with other things
Any more than a diseased man is
Cured by ignoring his sickness.

It's the only thing I know to be true:
That things persist.
That things endure.
That things resound.
That things collide.

> Like great celestial bodies
> Which are left changed, be them
> Larger or smaller or merely
> Altered in course.

And that these are all the same.
Who was it who said that God is an earthquake?
If he is right, we are each of us a tremor.

Once a geologist, Harold Strauss now studies that peculiar rock that rattles about in his head. He and his husband are retired, and they spend their days enjoying coffee on the patio and occasionally writing poetry together

Kintsugi – Merril D. Smith

My young body broken,
my soul flew
high above the pain,

resurfacing in dreams
with limbs ready,
in flight or fight responses

that fade into acceptance,
knowing I am bound together
by scars,

fragments glued together
not camouflaged, but gilded--
my before and after joined.

Merril D. Smith is a historian and poet. Her poetry and stories have appeared recently in Rhythm & Bones, Vita Brevis, Streetlight Press, Ghost City, Twist in Time, Mojave Heart Review, Wellington Street Review, Blackbough Poetry, and Nightingale and Sparrow.

Another Storm – Phillip Knight Scott

The hands on the clock
slowly orbit the pale, dull face,
seemingly unaware

that the snow brought
a chill (or
at least a hint.)

The sun almost
shone as babies blinked,
staring at nothing

a general malaise that
lay beneath bubbles and
banana pudding breath.

Yes
snow covers the grass
and

a cold chill echoes through
the last

of a winter storm that turned whatever
we had planned black and cold,

echoes.

Depression cries out
through the seemingly endless black
(where noise blinds us,
while

not so long ago
this all made sense).

Amid the senselessness
of another terrifying flash
of lightning –
of the fury

that flares for an instant
then recedes

to background noise – we
find solitude, short

of understanding.

Phillip Knight Scott is a native of Durham, North Carolina, where he lives and writes poetry. Though writing poems since childhood, he's only at age 39 published his first collection of poems, PAINT THE LIVING, PLANT THE DEAD. His poems have appeared in numerous publications including Galway Review, Vita Brevis Press, Olive Skin, Spillwords, and others.

Drops - Stacey Z Lawrence

Days old, colic
night
after night, I go to her,
viridescent onesie
pickled in sweat and piss.

I unsnap
snatch, replace, rewrap
reach for her drops, clutch,
squirt three into the wall of her cheek,
she retreats, breathes deep,
appeases herself
to sleep.

Days left, cancer
spews
into long, sallow days.
No more quarts of therapy
chemo-ing through
cell and marrow.

The vomiting
is over,
oxygen tank
no longer
needed, euthanized
that breathless old dog.

You are a shroud now, swaddled in
white, your bed, a mechanical
monster snarling in our living room.
I curl like a fetus by your
feet, rest between your
songs of quietus with

my little Pasteur pipette
I am your hospice,
dripping death
open mouth.

Stacey Z Lawrence teaches Poetry and Creative Writing in Northern New Jersey. Her work can be seen in Chaleur, Dream Noir, Black Fox, Vita Brevis and others. She was long- and short-listed for the Fish Poetry Prize 2019 and received the Lustgarten Foundation best poem prize in 2017.

In Memory of My Father - Shalini Pattabiraman

A bell rings in my memory
all echoes boomerang to that point of no return
and come back, collapsing
into dust of noise
shattering glass
like ripples jumping off water
when the rock
cuts into the surface
making kinetic all that was inert.

Held within these
I glide into the locked memory
unwinding the yarn tightly holding
onto your story
where you hold your frame
strapped to a spine
with sinews sewing
bone to muscle
as it falls loose.

Weak-limbed and frail
you pick up pieces of yourself
stick them with glue,
sealing them inside an envelope
posting it to the future
where I receive it one day.
I don't know what to do with the past?
How can I assemble all that was taken or lost?
How do I find my way to you?

How can I bring you back home
when home was there with you in it
and then you were gone
and we lost the definition of home
along with walls that made it concrete.
We have since been fixing pieces to a puzzle
matching soil to the limb, ash to the bone,
root to the muscle and there it grows

-a tiny tree, its leaves pages from your history!

Shalini is a traveler who hasn't quite found the words that help her describe who she is and where she belongs! A lot of what she writes is an attempt at negotiating meaning and coming to an understanding of the 'self'. She currently lives and teaches English at a secondary school in Scotland.

Demensch - Jean Fineberg

Mensch: German for Human
Demensch: to remove what makes us human

My mother sits, tiny, in her wheelchair
Her regal head held high
Her nubilous eyes wander,
seeking a landing strip

She forgets she was a dancer
but her muscles, like stronger children, remember
Her biography is written in disappearing ink -
black, blue, gray, white, gone

We think there's nobody there, but she is listening
"What's demensch," she asks
I flounder, and settle on
"When you forget things"

"Are you my mom?" she asks
- more floundering. "Yes," I say
"You were the mom and I was the daughter,
now I'm the mom and you're the daughter."

I have sampled dementia
It's that dream where you try to call but the numbers disappear
You head for home, but you take the wrong bus
Lost, always lost

Jean Fineberg is a jazz musician with a master's degree in Psychology, who teaches at a music conservatory. Her father was a poet. She recently unearthed a book of her poems written when she was eight. Jean received seven music composition residencies, and between writing music scores, she writes poems

Protection - Judith Capurso

Don't ask me again
to taste what others have tasted.
The flavors you changed so easily
turn bitter in my mouth
as I was learning not to swallow.
Don't ask me again
to hurt you
just to protect myself.
When I take up that wounded child
I give up the man.
 Don't ask me again
using touches that draw me.
In a dome of ice I wander
and your warm hand deceives me.
Kiss me goodbye now.
I go off into a wilderness
that is safer
than you.

Judith Capurso writes and works in the Catskill Mountains. In and out through daughter, sister, wife, mother, aunt, waitress, librarian, teacher, caregiver, script reader, and archivist, she continues to "stumble along between the immensities." Her work has been published in the ARAS online poetry portal, Psychological Perspectives, the BeZine: ezine & blog "Waging the Peace," and the Earth/Psyche issue of the Jungian Society of Scholarly Studies.

Water Levels - Alex Dreppec

We talk about our dead.
Everything is part of different times now.
We talk about water levels,
funeral blessing ceremonies and grave inscriptions.
We talk about water levels,
grave decorations and thank you cards.
Once I may have used these words
without knowing what they meant.

We talk about water levels,
what's your level, which is mine.
An image in a frame.
Objects everywhere.
We talk about our dead,
about what's over now
and about the lack of words,
we talk about water levels.

This picture is now a part of yesterday.
This song is now a part of yesterday.
Nevertheless, a part of me believed
I could talk to her afterwards.
We talk about our dead,
we talk about sea levels,
we talk about water levels,
what's your level, which is mine.

Alex Dreppec, German author with publications in German (Europe) and English (all five continents) and other languages.

"Wilhelm Busch" Prize 2004. Regular author of Parody on Impression (New York) and Das Gedicht, the biggest poetry journal of Europe. Invented the "Science Slam", an internationally spread event format where scientists present their own research.

My Mother's Secret – Linda Imbler

I found my mother's secret
tucked away in a
drawer beneath some bras,
after she had gone away,
inside five boxes
of feminine pads.
Pills of all descriptions
without prescriptions,
such a canny mind.
What I first thought as gross forethought,
in fact was brilliant,
the elegance of her secrecy.
All these years of mindful outlet
with numbness as the goal met.
She, closeting her pain,
keeping the pretense of
a younger woman's necessity
when in fact, no younger woman could harbor
so many years of ache.

*Linda Imbler has four published poetry collections and one hybrid
e-book of short fiction and poetry. She is a Kansas-based Pushcart
Prize and Best of the Net Nominee.*

Forgotten - Shalini Pattabiraman

In memory of my uncle and everyone else who lost a part of their core identity and self in the 1990 exodus of Kashmiri pundits from Kashmir.

Forgotten is a soft word
that curls up in your sleep
like the dream you saw
but can't remember
no matter how it gnaws at your skull
pounding it to pulp
with a sliver of a bone broken
somewhere,

where forgotten,
lies the new leaf
we turned over, promising
to never go back
and rewrite the history
of our lives
the one we left behind
putting the nail on an ancient
door to a house
we left, a long time ago
as if it were a coffin for living memories.

Forgotten, lies the thin skin
on your bones
shimmering in my memory
like the scales of a fish

flopping in the sunlight
when out of water.

Yet, you tread into that cold water
without fins and gills and tail
wanting to claim the irresistible solitude-
your minute of peace
in the ripples within,
that flopping fish tenderly held
in the cup of your hands while
your insane desire to become
what you aren't was never forgotten by me.

Forgotten was the taste of the kahva
simmering in the samovar
as shivering you gulped cups of it
soaking the heat of cinnamon and saffron
reciting over and over, 'I'm a fish out of the water!
I can't breathe' when you landed in Delhi's winter.

Forgotten the lanes, the cobbled street
the bulwark, the walnut trees dotting
your window frame,
of the home you left behind
in the middle of the night
when bullets, fire and fear for your family
bore over the weight of life without Kashmir.

Forgotten, you lift off
the skin of the milk now gone cold
as you stir the tea
and ache for lost threads.

Your memory, a cobweb
of all that exists in the smell and feel
of things that no longer come to you
in Delhi because everything else that
could have brought it back
was left behind in Kashmir.

Forgotten, you mumble words
and tie yourself in knots
as sleep deprived you hear voices
in the night and cannot tell the story
you want to write.
So you write on your skin
digging with your nails the imprint of words
you struggle to remember
and chase in your dreams.

Shalini is a traveler who hasn't quite found the words that help her describe who she is and where she belongs! A lot of what she writes is an attempt at negotiating meaning and coming to an understanding of the 'self'. She currently lives and teaches English at a secondary school in Scotland.

End of Year Review – Kelly Jayne McCann

In the bones of November
the past is revealed.
The moments are etched
as time holds still.
By December,
the year will be dismembered,
ready to place,
piece by piece
on shelves of glass
and well polished wood.
Come Spring, you'll buy a ticket
to visit the museum
where memories sit,
still mostly fresh.
Scabs are forming though,
camouflaging wounds.
Some will never heal.
Each visit you'll pick away
until blood runs freely again.

Kelly Jayne McCann works and plays on the shores of Lake Champlain in Burlington Vermont. As a life coach she helps people reclaim their dreams and create more authentic lives. As an evolving poet, she's taking her own advice, finally freeing her voice and writing from the heart.

Rip Tide Ride – Pauline May

They are knee-deep in that hangdog
tangle of their mismatched words;
the ricocheting ragbag, that crazed
checkmate hurt that
needs to hurt.
They are fear and
fury fused.

The soothing shoe string
rhythms of routine
are gone.

Us kids are yelled at
to 'Get up to bed' though it's
only just after tea.
The all-time, non-stop,
hell-bent anger bounces through our
tight gutted breath, planting the pulsing
tapeworm of watchfulness
within us.

For this sharp time
the raw, white knuckle,
rip tide ride must run. Those
long-drawn-out scabs must
be scratched afresh.
They cannot help but
make damn sure our
very floorboards feel their pain.

Pauline lives in Sunderland, UK, with her husband and cat. She enjoys performing at spoken word events across the north east of England and further afield. She has had poems published in The Writers Cafe, YorkMix magazine, The Blue Nib, Not Your Mother's Breast Milk, and Orbis. In June she won a Mslexia Mini Max competition judged by Helen Mort.

Patterns – Steve May

After her husband died, she was never the same.
The little things seemed hollow. That one spoon
scraping the cereal dish sounded
scratchy, flat, empty.

No one to cook for now; herself she didn't
really count. Sometimes you'd catch her
staring out the window, transfixed,
as if she was not in the room. She wasn't.

She took up knitting again, but it was painful.
Had she'd lost the knack or was it that
she couldn't put her mind to it; twelve months
to wait for that fair-isle jumper of mine.

They'd been inseparable all those years.
Their life together had been patterned
with little time-tested rituals, piled
on each other like mortarless bricks.

But when the base collapsed, the pieces
crashed into painful shards of memory:
the cosy local, occasional bites to eat
in country pubs, fish & chips for Friday treats;

at home, the garden seen to, lightbulbs changed.
windows reached, But just as much, the coughs,
the snores, the shuffling feet. Above all, the sound
of two spoons chiming in flake-filled bowls.

Steve May, an Edinburgh Fringe First winner with Wigan Young People's Theatre, regularly performs poems and stories around the NE of England and further afield. He has had work published or placed in numerous magazines, anthologies and competitions, including winning the 2019 Shelter Poems for Home Competition.

Washup row - Matt McGee

There may be nothing sadder than the top row
at any track, field or rink, the seats right beside the announcer's
booth,
where the men and women whose former rapt attention
turned years ago from their pursuit of full-throttle sport
to the pursuit of healing, making doctor's appointments
and getting to the pharmacy before they close.

There's Bob, whose hockey equipment was still anchored
in the '70s, who'd passed up inline rollerblades for his beloved
quads
once the thing of Panda Parties and roller disco.
Now a torn ACL confines him to an Uber job
he feels fortunate to have.

And there's Cindy, whose brilliant soccer career
came to a slow halt, like a landing jumbo jet, first
with the marriage to a man who wouldn't have anything
put before him, then insisted that nothing be put before their
kids, and finally after she lawyered her way out of his grasp
Cindy blew out a knee in her third season of adult league,
a tear that would keep her from running like the speed
of the wind she remembers too well.

But then there's Barry, who doesn't sit in the top row
but is only a row up from the field. You can't miss him,
shiny wheat-colored curls and arms of rope, when he leans forward
the v-neck of his t-shirt reveals the scar left by a cardiologist,
the one that's almost healed, the one his rehab partner says
should let him come back in about eight weeks.

It's a day I'm looking forward to,
and I'll try not to treat him like a glass figurine
because I know Barry wouldn't want it that way,
and he didn't work this hard just to be treated like
another refugee from an old-timer's game.

Matt McGee writes in the Los Angeles area. In 2019, his stories have appeared in Poetic Diversity, Gnashing Teeth, Octillo, Biograph and 'The Rebirthing Shed' currently appears in Zimbell House's "1929" anthology. When not typing he drives around in a vintage Mazda and plays goalie in local hockey leagues.

industrial garden - J.A. Carter-Winward

i asked an artist how much for his
      eternal metal flowers and his reply was
along the lines of too much.

so i bought the regular kind, the kind that
      wilts after only a few days. the kind that
were plucked like a million others on the

same day, the same hour, the same garden
      and row. seeds from the same family, who
knew the short life story of each other and

each one, even those who were chosen for
      shops instead of grocers, or ones with petals,
too unruly to belong in a proper bouquet, so

they're brought home by someone whose hands
      spend all day plucking flowers, not small stringed
instruments as they sing soft-voiced tunes

to their brown-eyed baby girls. someone whose
      pockets have no loose change and the flowers,
simply a token for recipient and giver. i imagine

how they both smile with an intimate knowing—sly, word-
      less—smiles that almost demand a wink, a human
exchange that speaks to how small—and great—the price

such a slight, fragrant clutch
      costs us all.

J.A. Carter-Winward is an award-winning poet, literary novelist, playwright, musician, film/visual artist, and performer. Author of 11 books, her work has appeared in the anthology, We Will Be Shelter (Write Bloody Publishing), HSTQ, Desert Wanderings Literary Journal, and Vita Brevis. J.A. is also a contributing writer to several online publications, including Mad in America: Science, Psychiatry and Social Justice.

Pre-Op - John Jeffire

The hairnet is cute,
adorable French painter,
Lucille Ball chef,
a shoulder exposed
flowing electrode wires.
"We got this," she whispers,
but her eyes moisten.
The gurney wheels
unlock in an anvil jolt.
Her mouth forms the words
"I'm afraid" but I am quick
with a "We got this," knowing
all I've really got is the sliver
thinness of her hand
squeezed in mine.

I'm led back out
to the waiting pen.
It is nearly full but
no one is there.
Two chairs set face
to face form a bed.
I take my wife's jacket
from the plastic stow bag
and form a pillow.
I stuff the pillow beneath
my head, a sleeve hanging
loose, which I drape in
a bandage over my eyes.

John Jeffire was born in Detroit. His novel Motown Burning was named 2005 Grand Prize Winner in the Mount Arrowsmith Novel Competition and 2007 Gold Medal Winner for Regional Fiction in the Independent Publishing Awards. His first book of poetry, Stone + Fist + Brick + Bone, was a 2009 Michigan Notable Book Award nominee. Former U.S. Poet Laureate Philip Levine called the book "a terrific one for our city." His most recent poetry collection, Shoveling Snow in a Snowstorm, was published by the Finishing Line Press in 2016.

The Baltimore Batechism – Thomas M. McDade

In the Boston 9th, Pierce fans
Stephens looking, Jackie drills
a single to right. Turk Lown,
master of many pitches takes
the mound. What a name!
Malzone manages a sickly slow
roller to Fox; luckily no turn
of 2 due to Jackie speed. Sammy
White unceremoniously ends
the contest with a swinging strikeout.
Amen. Score 3 to 1 like the Baltimore
"Batechism": "We cannot fully understand
how the three Divine Persons are one, and
the same God, because this is a mystery."
No puzzle here: obvious lack of timber.
What the heck, tomorrow a clean slate, sins
of omission swept clean. Like a couple of days
after failing to speak up in class when you would
have been the only one knew the answer or backing
down from a bully, take a week or more though.
If only Boston could had tied it up; I would have
appreciated the extra innings, possible redemption
"joyful tidings as written in the "Batechism."
Nun playing eighth grade be laying a hard
tag over my two blasphemies—Shhhh.

Thomas M. McDade is a 73-year-old resident of Fredericksburg, VA, previously CT and RI. He is a graduate of Fairfield University, Fairfield, CT. McDade is twice a U.S. Navy Veteran serving ashore at the Fleet Anti-Air Warfare Training Center, Virginia Beach, VA and at sea aboard the USS Mullinnix (DD-944) and USS Miller (DE / FF 1091).

Alone – Carson Pytell

I was nursing a soda and waiting for my sub
When she walked in and placed her order: two slices.
She sat down at the table across from me
And we made eye contact. She smiled some.
There were stains on my jacket.

Then, though, after my number was called
And I sat back down, I looked back at her
And she was still looking at me. I smiled
Then made a joke to my friend, who was
Sitting right beside me. She laughed.

I should have said something then,
Anything. But my friend began talking,
So I didn't. And a minute later she jumped up
And kissed her boyfriend. His watch got caught in her hair.
They grabbed their pizza and drove off in a fast car.

Carson Pytell is a poet and short fiction writer living in a very small town in upstate New York. His work has previously appeared or is forthcoming in such publications as Vita Brevis, Literary Yard, Leaves of Ink, Revolution John, Corvus Review, Gideon Poetry Review, Poetry Pacific, Futures Trading and Former People.

Bad Weather – Philip Pholeros Porter

The wind's in an agitated state this morning.
Annoying everyone.
Prodding, poking, coming
from different directions,
even aggravating
the variegated hedge
that jiggers and fidgets along the high school fence;
Medusa on a bad
hair day; mum off the smokes.

Dust, of no account, I bounce off
her swirls, her bleak pathology.
Unafraid, I land somewhere safe.
Her anger sated, I wait, content,
for the next mood to land me near,
far or miss me altogether.

Philip Pholeros Porter (previously Philip Porter) is an Australian poet of Greek and British origin. He is published in magazines and journals in Australia, Britain, New Zealand and the USA. He convenes the North Shore Poetry Project (NSPP) facilitating workshops, readings and Poetry dinners. He has co-edited collected works of the NSPP, "A Patch of Sun" and "The Intimacy of Strangers"

Liberation – Kelly Jayne McCann

I fold inward
Crunching bone against bone
Shredding muscle
Tearing ligaments
Liberating the cells
that hold my secrets
They fall
softly and quietly
to the ground
Fragments of me
in little piles
Ready to be reassembled
by the conservator of souls

Kelly Jayne McCann works and plays on the shores of Lake Champlain in Burlington Vermont. As a life coach she helps people reclaim their dreams and create more authentic lives. As an evolving poet, she's taking her own advice, finally freeing her voice and writing from the heart.

Kin Kelli 4: Creed– Katy Santiff

Who can tell me where she's living at ease?
Is she cobbled into the willow's boot,
or in the leaf-rustling rush of the breeze?
Is she yawning in the long-nameless vine
that stretches its neck to lick summer light?
Hibiscus bloom, she's folding in at night?
Does she chitter to me in squirrel song–
message so short when meaning is long?
Is she sleeping dark/cold, or does she glow?
She must reside inside warm nights. She grows
petals over thorns below. What a rose.
But me–until I'm tucked in hallowed muck,
just a carbonic creed, I'll bide a seed,
and one day root new feet below the weeds.

Katy Santiff has written poetry in various forms all her life. A fan of meter and rhyme, she loves lines that hypnotize the reader with their sound. She believes in densely packed poems, preferring them to be mouthfuls when read aloud. A lifelong Marylander, she loves waterside living, and currently lives in Annapolis, Maryland. Her works have been published in Vita Brevis, Spillwords Press, and Uppagus Magazine.

Farewell - Suzanne Cottrell

Her teary, soft azure eyes still twinkled
as she lay motionless in bed.
For months she fought relentlessly
enduring excruciating headaches,
nauseousness, chemotherapy,
radiation treatments, and
decreased strength and mobility.
She grasped my hand for the last time
knowing she needed to say good-bye.
Her eyes blinked as she gently squeezed my hand.
She graciously relinquished her life.
Cancer took her body, but
now heaven possesses her soul.

Suzanne Cottrell lives with her husband and three dogs in Piedmont North Carolina. An outdoor enthusiast and retired teacher, she enjoys writing, reading, knitting, hiking, and Pilates. Her poetry has appeared in journals such as Avocet, Plum Tree Tavern, Poetry Quarterly, and The Remembered Arts Journal. She was the recipient of the 2017 Rebecca Lard Poetry Award, Prolific Press.

Survivor's Guilt – Taylor Ashley King

I'm sorry about the hydrangeas blooming across your chest,
I wish they sprouted against mine instead.
You deserved endless fields of daisies and sunflowers and petunias,
And instead these dark, venomous red intruders forced their sprout.
The seeds which you gathered upon your soil were meant for me;
I think you know that, but yet
You still leaped at the chance to plant those wicked seeds as your own.
Your eyes are glowing with the color I feared most,
The pinks and oranges of the sky settling at the surface.
I pray with all I have that there are just a few seeds left,
So that I can let the wicked flowers sprout across my body as well,
As it isn't fair that only you must endure the unwilling garden,
That only you are forced to view the hues of nightbreak.
I grip tighter to the stems that bleed through gravel of fleece and yarn,
But they continue to thrive at unfathomable rates,
stronger and brighter than my trembling hands can contain.
The petals upheave and pour across the linoleum beneath,
Until the pinks and oranges turn to a choking obsidian.
I unwillingly water the garden which grows much slower,
Now that you cannot grasp at the roots.
Gardeners finally arrive to trim back the sprawling blossoms,
Minutes too late,
As I beg them to try harder.
They toss the hydrangea field into a bag,
As they are now nothing but miles of red flowers and halcyon,
For compost so that more of these dastardly flowers can bloom in others.

"At least the seeds only grew upon one chest and not two"
"Carry on so those plants did not invade in vain,
And feel blessed that you are able to apologize"
But they do not understand how we shared everything,
Yet in the end we shared nothing at all.
I lay coated in the petals long after they're gone.
—*for my love who never knew*

Taylor Ashley King is a graduate of San Jose State University with dreams of writing for television. She is working toward her teaching credentials in English, while working part-time in a local library. She spends her free-time writing comedy sketches and trying salvage meals prepared without recipes or measurements.

Somewhere in the Mountains – Harold Strauss

The American woke
His fire crackling in the cold air
A figure, pottering about in the fog.

And then a musket coughed
Flame and led through the night
And the figure slopped into the mud.

Somewhere in the mountains
A hunter yipped, his barrel smoking.
He'd shot a native who brought only gifts.

And a million more would follow.

Once a geologist, Harold Strauss now studies that peculiar rock that rattles about in his head. He and his husband are retired, and they spend their days enjoying coffee on the patio and occasionally writing poetry together.

From One Widow to Another – Erina Booker

widowed bird above
me in the jacaranda
tree, a dark splotch
in the lace and tatting
of fronds and twigs
and I am there
with her, delicately
balanced, shifting
weight imperceptibly,
so as not to
plummet like
Icarus, break
the bough, the bird
the webbed support
to merely fulfil
gravity.

Erina Booker is a Sydney-based poet. Her life revolves around poetry, from publishing books and contributing to journals, to recitals at public events and presentation of seminars. She was delighted to present a seminar to a class of students in another country via the medium of Flip-Grid. She contributes ekphrastic poems to art galleries, works regularly with artists and craftspeople, and supports poetry within her local community.

Autumn Healing - Gabriela M.

this autumn heals all my pains
on top of the old mountains it lights fires
my youth, the sweetness of grapes
my arms stretched beyond the veins of the islands
talismans, handkerchiefs made out of gold
my eyes, algae of skies
I walk in the clouds with this autumn
in beds of sunflowers I sleep
the chill of the rivers follows young deer
I hold at my breast the youngest of children

this autumn stretches purple shadows
over unending fields of sweet corn and hurt souls
it brings from the depth the lacustrine goddess
who heals all wounds with yesterday's mirth
I kneel in front of this autumn
waters are falling between your fingers and mine
and every drop of rain
washes the mud from my aching shoulders

Gabriela M. is a US university professor and author of three novels. Her poetry was published by Spillwords Press, Vita Brevis, Gioielli Rubati Poetry:32, Tuck Magazine, and other journals and newspapers. She was selected "Author of the Month" (April 2019) at Spillwords. Her work was included in the anthology America's Emerging Poets Southeast Region (Z Publishing House, 2018) and Florida's Best Emerging Poets 2019 (Z Publishing House, August 19, 2019). Christina Schwarz, the author of the New York Times Bestseller "Drowning Ruth," on Gabriela's poetry: "With lush language and lavish imagery, Gabriela M. evokes a fantastic world ripe with emotion."

Soldier - Linda Imbler

What he saw.
What he did-
indecent and horrific.
He talks about it
in that circular fashion
that avoids facing reality.
That would break him.
So he skirts around
what was required, then, to do the job.

What else rents him in two,
conjunction,
love of one's brothers,
dehumanizing one's enemies,
in corresponding time and space.

Before and after was easy.
Intellectualize the task,
the aftermath not cerebral.
Feeling it is worse,
yet not having done it
would have been the atrocity.

The tearing does not mend.
Repellent memories
overshadow knowledge
of crucial guardianship.
He'll live out

the rest of his days,
in pain and not whole.

*Linda Imbler has four published poetry collections and one hybrid
e-book of short fiction and poetry. She is a Kansas-based Pushcart
Prize and Best of the Net Nominee.*

Grief - Sharon Arthur

You left behind
a playbill of "Midsummer Night's Dream"
to show me that fairies do exist
and meddle in men's every turn and twist
as they plot their nightly scheme
on the moonbeams that you divined

you wanted me to know
the glory of the pauper's stage
where pennies are thrown like roses at the stars
the beauty of the musical bars
written on your soul's page
before you disappeared into the universal flow

you wanted me to hold
your words written on old parchment wood
of oak trees where our memories join
and I sprang from your root's loin
where with you Apollo once stood
giving me his healing gold

I try to recover from your death
but still I hear your lungs expand
in every dust speck of this home
you settle like gold dust over my loam
as you touch me with your tender hand
building my brick house with your breath.

Sharon Arthur has a B.S. degree in therapeutic recreation and a B.F.A. degree in painting and printmaking. She had a successful 20-year career as an artist and a painter in oils on canvas, with a commercial fine art gallery in Duck, North Carolina. She was a caregiver for her elderly parents for 10 years until their passing. In 2019 she independently published a poetry book, The Wind Softly Murmurs Poems of Family Love and Loss. "Grief" is previously published from that book.

Videos You've Kept of Me - Jonah Carlson

It is dreamless sleep, the end of a film.

The subject is born with a click and is tortured sixty times a second, paralyzed within a suit of
flesh. You cut it up, run it back, start it up, watch the bound bird gasp for air again.

Strings yank: that's the song of the spinning ballerina always too tightly wound. She is forced to
scream her notes, to die with the last picture—to cease to exist.

Yet still I threw myself into those rectangular prisms. I cannot tear the seams—I am incapable, a
shell of human matter automated by your own hand.

Yesterday was my funeral. You were there with some friends of mine and afterwards, behind a
willow tree on the far side of the cemetery, you reincarnated me, but I didn't remember.

Jonah Carlson is a young poet living in Kaysville, Utah. His work has been published in Leaves of Ink and Vita Brevis. He plans to study history in college and to continue writing in his free time.

Without Wheels – Sterling Warner

Absinthe lips; cloudy mind preparing to flee,
milky perceptions push past clarity,
head hangs over a Moulin Rouge dreamscape,
hands grasp cards,
siblings laugh before I
etch a metamorphic moment
on their minds forever,
my chainsaw mumbling, fracturing
early morning tranquility
without intention,
seizure giving birth to a life its own,
moving on a journey as definite as the
Ford station wagon hospital haul,
family members wondering what I'd remember.

Images blurry, confounding:
vegetarians munching down on mandrake roots,
butterfly mandalas miscuing prosperity and good luck
Victoria's Secret sales girls wearing
shrink-wrap dresses and paper jewelry,
their credit card figures exquisitely braced
against tofu pocket books,
tossing cell phones like trinkets into wishing wells; all
stability's suspect, control as uncertain as
legs shimmying up greased lampposts;
life without wheels, untouchable—beyond
eight-fold paths or twelve-step programs—
alters meaning, builds temporal mountains
from breadcrumbs that sink like
Canada sucked into the belly of Florida.

Short breaths, muted screams
cry out for examination,
mouth rot dry as Denver's throat
seeks moisture, epileptic acceptance, lifelong endurance,
the dignity afforded silent winds championing
Don Quixote's ethics, chivalric code, or family values,
ideals forever laced like gauntlets, thrown at my feet
lasting quagmire of mucus, guilt, shame.

Sunshine's not on any astrological chart,
psychic reading, job description;
charity's no host to lives without wheels.

A writer, poet, and educator, Sterling Warner's poetry and fiction have appeared in dozens of literary magazines, journals, and anthologies, including In The Grove, The Flatbush Review, Street Lit: Representing the Urban Landscape, American Mustard, Chaffey Review, Leaf By Leaf, and The Atherton Review. Warner also has published five collections of poetry, including Shadowcat, Edges, Rags and Feathers, and Memento Mori Redux. Warner currently lives and writes in Union, WA and is working on a collection of fiction.

Pinking Dock - Stephen Kingsnorth

Shades to mask the eyes,
uncertain if corporeal,
the filtered sight is grey
in a ghostly dusky way.

So frequent iterations,
was my story ever true
or was it built of buried fears
emerging into light?

When Mum created tapestry,
used her pinking shears,
I wondered if my tale had frayed,
border less well defined.

My sentence led to his,
I watched his baleful eyes;
had I elaborated,
added lustre for the cause?

Was my imagination fired,
atonement down the road?
His panting in my ears
as we raced home after school.

We talked and walked in woods,
the briars scratched my back,
a bed of nettles left me stung,
while bared flesh wore their weals.

That day he soothed my angry skin,
rubbed broad rumex on my flesh;
the next arrest, stayed closed by dock
then only I could leave.

My mother needed Dad around
to bring his wages in,
so father never went to court,
uncle paid the price in jail.

*Stephen Kingsnorth, retired to Wales from ministry in the
Methodist Church, has had pieces accepted by Nine Muses Poetry,
Voices Poetry, Eunoia Review, Runcible Spoon, Ink Sweat and
Tears, The Poetry Village, The Seventh Quarry, Gold Dust, From
the Edge, and Allegro.*

Who's Left to Row the Boat - Ivor Steven

The storms are too many to count
Emotional lows had weathered me out
Her journey with MS was a struggle
How much lower could our lives sink

After fourteen years of our battles, I suffered a Stroke
An ambulance came, my brain was in a boat
Floating out to sea, overboard and panic-stricken
I wasn't swimming, barely awake, and drifting
I had fallen, nothing was working, and not talking
She's crying, I'm sobbing, my heart is dying
And who's left to row the boat, I'm thinking
I was jabbed with a needle and silently sleeping

I awoke a day later, in hospital, feeling wasted
My face was limp, mouth parched, was that death I tasted
My mind was active, I thought, where is she
I knew I was bad; the room was all blurry to me
Strong anxieties had set in, I needed to know
Nurses came to me, I pleaded, I wanted to go
"Help me to see her, just give my bed a tow
Please let me go, before I'm covered in snow"

Ivor is a part-time plumber, former Industrial Chemist, and now a serious writer of poetry. He has had numerous poems published, in on-line magazines such as, Vita Brevis. SpillWords, Drabble, Wolff Poetry Journal, Festival of Poetry, Slasher Monster Magazine, and Fae Corps Publishing. He is an active member of the Geelong Writers Inc.

Our Pain Won't Go Away – Walt Page

My pain is pretty constant now
It's with me all the time
I just want to go to sleep
And wake up feeling fine

The pain pills take the edge off
But they don't stop the ache
And even if I fall asleep
It comes back when I wake

Like many others that I know
I live with pain each day
And now the politicians want
To take our pills away

"We must protect them from themselves"
The politicians say
I think they need to take our pain
And bear it for a day

The regulations that they want
Will only cause more pain
But they don't really give a damn
They don't even know our names

Walt is a romantic old rock drummer and US Air Force veteran living the country life in Tennessee and writing poetry on love, life, music and whatever comes to mind. Owner of Teaka, a palomino paint mare, Glacier, a registered Blue Roan Gypsy Vanner gelding and 10 rescue dogs. Published on Visual Verse, Vita Brevis, and Slasher Magazine.

Unwound – Ken Gierke

hope
a lie lost in fragments, scattered
like bits of a broken shell

misery
a watch left unwound,
merely witnessing time

defeat
grief anticipated,
fulfilled by default

overturned, untended,
a boat left to the elements
will not hold a net,
fish another day

Ken Gierke started writing poetry in his forties but found new focus when he retired. This also gave him new perspectives, which are woven into his writing, primarily in free verse and haiku. His poetry has been featured at Vita Brevis, The Ekphrastic Review, Eunoia Review, and Amethyst Review.

PAIN

RENEWAL

Long sleeps the summer in the seed;
Run out your measured arcs, and lead
The closing cycle rich in good.

- Alfred, Lord Tennyson, In Memorium

RENEWAL

Earth is God - Naida Mujkić

It's been 15 days since I came
To the land of Aborigines, at the end of the world,
but I still haven't seen any Aborigine
At souvenir shops smiling Chinese women are selling
Aboriginal items, bracelets, colourful bowls and
embroidered purses, some dead plants and kangaroo landscapes
Saying that right that item which caught
My eye, right that one, is a true Aboriginal symbol
Leave me alone, woman, my head is full of symbolism
But I'm not telling her that
Instead, I'm asking her: "Where are the Aborigines"
"They aren't here, they're up in the mountains" says the shop
assistant
So I went up to the mountains, the blue mountains
And I saw snow on mimosas and magnolia trees
Looking like a veil, and confused fern
And wild cockatoo birds
Waddling on one leg like comedians
And a tiny tea house at the edge of the road
Serving English tea
Fuck, I don't want tea, where are the Aborigines?
"They aren't here. They're in the desert" said the foresters
So I went to the desert
With my eyes covered with a piece of bed sheet, other parts
I might need
When I told my mother where I was
She thought I was joking
"You're not right in your head" she told me, and I
confirmed, but nothing could be done now

I'm lighting a cigarette in despair, the sun is scorching
Like Your Word god forbid
I'm looking at the cracked earth Aborigines
Made love with, because earth is god,
I'm watching and I'm not looking for anything anymore

Naida Mujkić, PhD. Her work has appeared in literary journal and anthologies around the world. So far, she published five books of poetry and one book of lyrical prose. She has participated in several international poetry and literature festivals.

Cicada - Karla Whitmore

I was a number today
Renewed my photo ID
In a blue and red cocoon
Of auto announcements
Ticket 41 proceed to counter three
I tried an empathetic smile
Aimed at the man beside
But he declined to reciprocate
Retreating to that protected space
When faced with anonymity -
So poignantly depicted
In a story by Shaun Tan
Succinctly called Cicada
Of a small grey suited insect
In a basement toiled 17 years
Until retirement came then
On the office roof top terrace
Shed his dreary outer shell
Revealing a vibrant free spirit
Took wing for a distant green forest -
I think I glimpsed stoic Cicada
As I emerged into the sun

Karla Whitmore lives in Sydney, Australia and is retired from working in professional association and university administration and as a book editor. She researches and writes on Australasian stained glass windows and belongs to a local poetry writing group.

Homarus americanus – Shanna Maybright

My daughter, she blended into the storm and sea
While tossing the Atlantic between her feet.
Clouds as black as her grandfather. Waves just as wrinkled.
Sea just as ancient. Youth a contradiction.

Africa is my due north. Even from this coast,
I feel my soul point back home. And then she turned to it,
Like I always had, and stared off real solemn.

I'd have taught her of chains and ships, but I never understood it
myself.
So I just loved her. And she loved me. And history for us is history.

And then she stopped and bent over and pulled something from the
deep.
As if it'd been waiting. As if she'd been searching.

If he were still here, he'd have watched her and said:
Homarus americanus! And told us how it lived. How it bred. How it
ate.
How the ghettos aren't as bad as the lobster's way.

How "food stamps ain't nothing to chopped eyestalks and pitched
rears"

But he's gone. So she came to me, lobster dangling in hand.
And placed it at my feet. Where she used to crawl and hug
When the air went out. Because the floor was cooler.
And Mom, well, she was warm but warm with love.

And she looked up and asked: "How deep is the Atlantic?"
And the whole world sung through me.
"Deep as all, darling. The deepest deep."

Shanna Maybright is a loving mother of two children. Everything else comes secondary.

The Amaryllis - Theresa Burns

Still clap-closed, still podded like hands
in prayer, the amaryllis
my friend gave me for Christmas
is still unbloomed. More sun,
she suggests, and a thorough
weekly watering. I look for a window
on the first floor where it streams
in strong, but there is none.

What I need is a room
like the one I'd find my mother
snoozing in, late afternoon
in my growing-up house, the sun a wall-length
heat lamp, fierce healer of aches,
eraser of worries, where for twenty minutes each day
she could close her eyes, and open,
and dream of anything but us.

Theresa Burns' poetry, reviews, and nonfiction have appeared in The New York Times, Prairie Schooner, Bellevue Literary Review, America Magazine, New Ohio Review, The Journal of the American Medical Association (JAMA), and elsewhere. She was nominated for a Pushcart Prize in 2018, and her chapbook of poems, Two Train Town, was recently published by Finishing Line Press. A long-time book editor in New York and Boston, she has taught writing at Seton Hall University, The Fashion Institute of Technology, and the 92nd Street Y.

River Man – Harold Strauss

When I see the sunlight filter through the foliage
And fall across your face
I think back to the 80's
And the river where we met.

I had my Walkman by Panasonic on my chest.
It was that RQ-SX91 in Gold that you called "haughty."
And I told you there's no sense in playing Mahler
On anything less.

You laughed at me. And, as if in retaliation, I asked what you were reading
But you never showed me. You just dipped your feet into the river,
And launched into the water. Leaving your towel behind on the grass.

Still warm.

I watched you as I moved from my towel
To yours.
And I've been there ever since.

Once a geologist, Harold Strauss now studies that peculiar rock that rattles about in his head. He and his husband are retired, and they spend their days enjoying coffee on the patio and occasionally writing poetry together.

Holding Stones - Karen Shepherd

I did what I was told, that's what good girls did.
The pews and plaid skirts, the genuflecting,
the rosary beads between my fingers,
saying prayers for people far away,
for people I didn't know while daddy
gave mommy a black eye, while mommy
taught me about make-up and scarves,
while I practiced how to be quiet like in church.
　　　　I hold so many stones in my pockets
Grandma and grandpa were high society folks,
sipping gin and tonics with the right people,
then sending daddy to fetch them from bars
that he wasn't old enough to enter.
Most houses had gardens planted with sorrow, joy, loss, laughter.
Daddy's house was built on an estate seeded with anger.
　　　　I hold so many stones in my pockets.
Now, he holds Mom's hand as we walk around the pond.
He says he could have been a better father, better husband.
I tell him I love him, and he shows me how
to throw a pebble so that it skips across the surface.
He says it's the spin that keeps it stable while it bounces.
We readjust our angle and keep trying.
　　　　I hold so many stones in my pocket.

Karen Shepherd lives in Portland, OR where she enjoys walking in forests and listening to the rain. Her poetry and short fiction have been published in various online and print journals including most recently Elephants Never, Neologism Poetry Journal, Cirque Journal, and Mojave Heart Review.

Under Leaden Clouds - Jim Brosnan

In the silent
shadows
of a late
October evening,
I slip into
a used bookstore
where a golden
oldies station is playing
"Unforgettable"—
an unexpected flashback
of the first time
I saw you
as my daydreams
wander in a tangle
of wildflowers,
a landscape
of oak and pine
where sparrows
reveal something
about that summer
in Barcelona
where our footsteps
were barely heard.

Jim Brosnan's publishing credits include Nameless Roads (Moon Pie Press, 2019), a 2019 Pushcart Prize nomination, and over 500 poems most recently in the Aurorean, Crossways (Ireland), Eunoia Review (Singapore), Nine Muses Poetry (Wales), Strand (India), Voices of the Poppies Anthology (UK) and Scarlet Leaf Review (Canada).

Consider the Lily – William Sterne

Look at the birds of the air;
they neither sow nor reap nor gather into barns

And it is simple, I hear, to let go...

/(So you can breathe easy and
Unload the years of grief
That have settled between your
Shoulder blades and spread across
Your thighs

Consider the lily of the field, how they grow: they neither toil
nor spin

Because his hands are not there to rub
Them any longer. So the phantom pressures
Persist and bundle.
So they do. So they will.
Such is loss. Such is our endeavor.)\

...if only you give in, so living this way
Is always coming home.

William Sterne is not a poet, but a reader who was urged by his
husband to try his hand at verse. This is the result.

Picking Up the Sun - Graham Wood

Out of the silences that are myself
through a dream that loops and curls,
my dead father swims beneath sun-glint
on lagoon water, holding his breath
for time beyond count.

I sense rather than see him
know he's there beneath
the water like a shark, close
but dangerous no longer.
Bursting then to air, his head
and shoulders break the surface
in a thousand splinters of light;
bright beads of water
fall in cascade from his hair.

His smile is unfenced, open.
Against blue sky and palm trees
he rises from the warm lagoon
alive again and young, his wars
now always over, gold tooth
forever picking up the sun.

Graham Wood lives in Hornsby, New South Wales and has had poetry published previously in a range of Australian magazines and journals. He is currently working on putting together an initial collection of his poems.

The Birth - M. Taggart

It worked. He reached in back of his kayak,
felt the cool neck of a beer, pulled it from its
cardboard six-pack holder and placed it in his lap.
He liked the way the droplets slowly slid down the
glass bottle. He opened the beer and swallowed.
The current of the Connecticut River was guiding
him directly to the island beach where he would
sit in the warm sand and read his book. The mountain
was barely in view, he could just make out the cliffs.
The summer greenery on each side of the riverbanks
was full and beautiful. He was the only one on the river.
He'd take his time with this beer while he read his favorite
author. Days like this are worth remembering. She asked
him to move to Rhode Island with her. It had been a long
five years. But, it worked. He needed that time to file through
the torture, the abuse, the reality and how to best find
himself. He drank the beer with a full heart knowing
it was time to start a life with a new future. One that
his past couldn't hold down. Those ties were loosened,
understood, and cut. It was time and the beer tasted wonderful
as the words from the book filled his soul. The river water
was clear, he could see to the bottom where smooth sand was
waiting to be found for the first time. His kayak slid calmly
onto the beach. It was a long five years, but he knew himself
as well as he knew the trees out his window and the mountain
just ahead with the blue and grey cliffs. He chuckled thinking
about damaged sheetrock and about how accessible it is to repair.
"Tell life it can't," he thought.

Matt is a loving father and husband. Matt has been published in America's Emerging Literary Fiction Writers: Northeast Regions, 2019 (Z Publishing House), America's Emerging Horror Writers: East Region, 2019 (Z Publishing House), Massachusetts's Emerging Writers; An Anthology of Fiction, 2018 (Z Publishing House), Vita Brevis Press, The Drable, proletaria, and was nominated author of the month of June, 2018, on Spillwords Press. His short story "Bodies in the Basement" was nominated and elected publication of the month in the 13 Days of Halloween segment on SpillWords.

Kin Kelli 7: Blow – Katy Santiff

The furrowed fields rest in winter reserve.
Dozens of nubs reach through the corn-stalk rows
like stubble on our grandfather's chin, while
tobacco ghosts with nowhere to go
(and no one yet ready to let them in)
stoop in these old open barns in the snow,
tilting and lilting the bone-stilting wind.

You won't be the last one that we know who
dies, we are told, when they work hard to make
us think that this strange thing, blow by tougher
blow, is a scattering of seed, and what
we need is temperament enough to sow.
No. I think somewhere in fields there must be
millions of us, wound together like weeds,
flowering since it's rained. There, we sustain.

Katy Santiff has written poetry in various forms all her life. A fan of meter and rhyme, she loves lines that hypnotize the reader with their sound. She believes in densely packed poems, preferring them to be mouthfuls when read aloud. A lifelong Marylander, she loves waterside living, and currently lives in Annapolis, Maryland. Her works have been published in Vita Brevis, Spillwords Press, and Uppagus Magazine.

Pollen Path - Judith Capurso

Planting: it was still dark.
Earth cold but strangely,
not frozen.
So I dug.
Days short.
Nights too long even for sleeping.
Beginning to forget light,
warm, and birdsong.
But the towering pines spoke:
"We, too, were once too small to see...
all this was here..."
And green came.
And sun blew.
And pollen drifted powerfully
into the empty places
to begin it all again.

Judith Capurso writes and works in the Catskill Mountains. In and out through daughter, sister, wife, mother, aunt, waitress, librarian, teacher, caregiver, script reader, and archivist, she continues to "stumble along between the immensities." Her work has been published in the ARAS online poetry porta, Psychological Perspectives, the BeZine: ezine & blog "Waging the Peace," and the Earth/Psyche issue of the Jungian Society of Scholarly Studies.

Telogen Winter, 2010
- Oormila Vijayakrishnan Prahlad

The first leaf fell in October
coinciding with the flight
of the first skein of migrating geese
arrowing through the skies
their GPS set for warmer latitudes.

two days later I caught the first filaments
quivering, coming loose
falling from the edge of my hairline
in a week my hairbrush matted
a tangle of ebony strands
young roots with bulbous ends.

through the window by my bedside
in drug induced inertia
I watched the cherry tree
shed freely along with me
a companion in denudation.

by December the coursing molecules
of Tegretol in my bloodstream
swiftly ate through the withered remnants
of what was once my crowning glory.

by April, mercy prevailed
on the beach by the dunes
as I lay in remission
the seagulls called above the sonorous
lub dub of the ocean.

sunshine skimmed off my forehead
where the fine down of virgin hair
pushed its way up like the axillary buds
dotting the Okame cherry
full of promise, both tree and I
waiting to return
to our former lushness.

Oormila Vijayakrishnan Prahlad is a Sydney based artist, poet and pianist. She holds a Masters in English and is a member of Sydney's North Shore Poetry Project and Authora Australis. Her recent works have been published in Red Eft Review, Glass Poetry Journal's Poets Resist, Eunoia Review, Plum Tree Tavern, and several other literary journals.

Revival – Cynthia Pitman

-- dedicated to my beloved daughter, Rebecca Pitman

After the silence,
after the stillness,
after the emptiness,
small sounds begin
to creep back in.
They come one by one,
an insistent procession:
the clock ticking,
the faucet dripping,
the heater humming,
the dogs barking --
all of them, just the same,
just like before.
Step by step,
they steal their way
into my tomb,
the sarcophagus of silence
in which I try to seal myself
from their persistent call to life.
They surround me,
shout at me,
"Breathe!"
And I breathe.

(First published in Leaves of Ink)

Cynthia Pitman is a retired English teacher with poetry published in Vita Brevis Press, 3rd Wednesday One Sentence Poem Contest (finalist), Ariel Chart, Amethyst, Leaves of Ink, Right Hand Pointing, Ekphrastic, Adelaide, Quail Bell, Big Windows, and others, and with prose published in Dual Coast, Red Fez, and Saw Palm. Her poetry collection, The White Room, is forthcoming.

Your Heaven - J. Lynn Lunsford

I think about your heaven and I wonder
How it might look.
I'm sure it's not the one
From Sunday School, with golden streets and mansions.
Your heaven is more likely to have dusty roads
And maybe even scraps of paper and cigarette butts
Blown against a chain-link fence
In a barrio across the tracks, on the edge of town.

Your heaven will ring with children laughing,
Playing chase and spinning in tight circles
Until they crumple into heaps of giggles.
Your heaven will have tambourines and bubbles
And miles of clean walls
Awaiting transformation by tiny hands
Wielding fresh Crayola markers
Into promises of endless possibilities.

I think you'll have a hammock there that overlooks the river.
And you'll nap in the shade while the Cottonwoods
Hum hopeful wind songs.
Every day will be the restful hour before sunset
On replay
As the sky welcomes nightfall with a symphony
Of orange and red, painting majestic
Tapestries on towering summer clouds.

Did you know your heaven sometimes sends postcards?
Messages framed in wood and transmitted in still-life

Through colored glass
Refracting sunlight and gentle inspiration.
Or in your silhouette as you quietly follow
The windings of a prayer labyrinth etched
By the feet of pious pilgrims
Into the floor of a cathedral on a hillside in France.

I think about your heaven and I wonder
Where it is.
I know they say it's far away and nothing we can see.
But then I see you, the lone adult in forest of big-people legs
Kneel to share a moment
And maybe your tambourine and bubbles
With a child.
I think about your heaven and realize it's here.

Lynn Lunsford is a Fort Worth, Texas, writer. He works as a communications manager for the Federal Aviation Administration. Before joining the FAA in June 2009, Lunsford was aerospace editor for The Wall Street Journal. He was a member of a team of reporters whose work earned the Journal the 2001 Pulitzer Prize for Breaking News Reporting for coverage of the Sept. 11 attacks on the World Trade Center and the Pentagon. He writes poetry on an antique typewriter when nobody is looking.

My Mother's Voice - Charles Murray

I heard a voice from down the past of years
that spoke to me of righteous men and kings,
that never let me once forget my place
nor the hope to then aspire to greater things,
and through the hard travail that was her life
in the sacrifice of needs that were foregone,
she underwrote the victories I won
and claimed no prize but the fact of duty done.
How clear that voice, it calls to make me hear,
remember all the lessons that were learnt,
my place to foster peace and never fear
the consequence of failure or being spent,
but to rise again, much stronger than before,
and to wipe your feet when coming in the door.

Charles Murray lives and works in Sydney, Australia, and has been dedicated to creative writing and poetry since his student days over fifty years ago, and as a proactive peace-loving social justice activist, his poetry and memoir pieces have been published in anthologies and in the broadsheet, tabloid and magazine media throughout Australia and overseas.

The Edge of Time – Ann Christine Tabaka

And if I stand on the edge of time watching,
will the seeker find me there tomorrow?

Clouds drift beneath emerald peaks,
blocking out humanity.

Shall I witness the righting of all wrongs,
as the sun burns through the fog?
I await the coming of truth.

For I do not exist anymore,
I am just an apparition of my fantasy,
swimming through time and space.

Can tomorrow be a reality,
if it does not exist today?

Atop the pinnacle of imagined thought,
We reach for that which we cannot see.

All the while trying to understand
what beyond our crystal eyes,
vanishes in a wink.

So I stand and ponder thusly,
as wind carries me over the edge,
and the seeker takes my hand to guide.

Ann Christine Tabaka was nominated for the 2017 Pushcart Prize in Poetry, has been internationally published, and won poetry awards from numerous publications. She is the author of 9 poetry books. Christine lives in Delaware, USA. She loves gardening and cooking. Chris lives with her husband and three cats.

The Seed – Marsha Warren Mittman

"To see things in the seed, that is genius." Lao Tzu
The seed lies deep
Dormant from ageless beginnings
Buried within
Hidden, silent, unknown
Waiting
Patient
Cloaked with darkness
And unconscious density

Suddenly
An infinitesimally small ray,
The most slight sliver of light
!Slices! through density and darkness
Through unconsciousness
To gently prod seed from slumber

With promise of transcendence
Into glorious flowers...

Marsha Warren Mittman's humorous memoir, You Know You Moved to South Dakota from New York City WHEN... is forthcoming from Scurfpea Publishing. Her poetry, essays, and short stories have been published in America, Britain, Germany, and Australia. She's been awarded poetry/prose distinctions in the US and Ireland, and a writing residency at the Fairhope Center for the Writing Arts in Alabama.

A Stick – Dan A. Cardoza

Dawn is doing dawn, breaking.
At the bank of the river
there is oneness. It is all about a stick.
Not a Sequoia, or wooden sliver.

Today is not about reverence or devotion.
Not really. Tomorrow expects that.

The current is swift, an oily viscous of
dorsal and Caudal fins. It is swollen
in scales. They drift and shimmer,
cleave sun into shards. Mirror rainbows.

How perfectly the water cracks. It's a
free-for-all, a variable fish rodeo.

Again, again, again he begs. Until
the end of eternity? Once tired, the compromise,
until the river dries?

A warm fall evening fire, a crackle, a pop
a twitch. An ocean full of exhausted sticks.

Dan A. Cardoza's poetry, nonfiction, and fiction have met international acceptance. He has an M.S. degree in education from C.S.U.S. Most recently his work has been featured in Cleaver, Coffin Bell/2019 Anthology, Dime Show Review, Entropy, Gravel, New Flash Fiction Review, Poached Hare, Spelk, and Vamp Cat.

Riddle of Renewing – J. lewis

evergreen should always mean
a tree that doesn't lose its leaves
not deciduous, nor bare in winter

but then there comes this riddle—
where does the forest floor
find its deep carpet of needles
tapestry of life unwinding
in tans and browns and grays
on their way to humus
providing life for the next
generation of giants

here is the wisdom of the question—
that which would continue green
must daily release anything
everything no longer needed
forget yesterday's yearnings
focus on feeding the present
so tomorrow will not want

i would be an evergreen—
past deeds scattered on the wind
forgotten in favor of nurturing now
quietly letting the good i have done
become nutrient soil to my soul
and to those sheltered seedlings
springing up around me

(First published in The Gnarled Oak)

J. lewis is an internationally published poet, musician, and nurse practitioner. When he is not otherwise occupied, he is often on a kayak, exploring and photographing the waterways near his home in California. His first book of poetry and photography, "a clear day in october", was released in June 2016.

Encounter with a Kung Fu Master
- Karla Whitmore

You stand so effortlessly
synchronous mind and body forging
one indomitable spirit,
head reaching skyward, feet planted on earth
heart beating the pulse of life
the sound of the universe.

A vestigial memory stirs
though my body is no more young
of toes en pointe in pirouette
and fingers swan-like flexing
limbs and mind roused to choreograph
and reprise the dance of life.

Karla Whitmore lives in Sydney, Australia and is retired from working in professional association and university administration and as a book editor. She researches and writes on Australasian stained glass windows and belongs to a local poetry writing group.

Visiting With Chaos – Ali Grimshaw

Spills splattered the walls.
Counters filled with clutter,
multiple piles creating a new geography in the room.
There is a relief to cleaning it all away.
Everything in order. Repair and replace.
The seduction of a new cycle, sparkle of clean.
Free from marks of history.
What if we could sit with Chaos
for just a little minute?
Feel the wind in our ears.
Hearing her secrets of cleverness.
To soak in the learning of this undone space.
Before an opportunity is erased.
A past disinfected before she can author her story
from which the plot differs from
perpetual duplicating.

Ali Grimshaw is a hope rebel living in Portland, Oregon. Her poems have been published on Right Hand Pointing, Vita Brevis, Amethyst Review, and Ghost City Review.

Salvation - Megha Sood

Pain unravels at the mere fleeting touch
unworn like a ball of yarn
laid bare--
ready to be woven again
into something beautiful

something to embrace the pain
to shadow the apricity of the summer sun
my soul feverishly waits
for a warm winter morning

palms opened in relaxation
an end to this hamster on wheel routine
unknotted from the worries
with the serenity of a monk
under the half-opened eyelids

I mock and revere at the beauty
around me
as the petrichor from the recent rains
douses my soul
seeping every pore of my being
with its fragrance

With every passing moment
the bowl is getting filled with the generous rain
drop by drop
a sign of synchronicity;
a sign of salvation,

for the parched beaks of sparrows
lining up my courtyard wall.

Megha Sood is a member and editor at Sudden Denouement, Whisper and the Roar, and editor at Ariel Chart. Her 300+ works have been featured in FIVE:2: ONE, Better than Starbucks, Foliate Oak, Dime show review, etc. Works featured in 20 anthologies by the US, Australian and Canadian Press. Two-time state-level winner of the NAMI NJ Poetry Contest 2018/2019.

Unnoticed - Jim Brosnan

I no longer linger
at the edge of prairie,
no longer
study
cloud formations
receding in the distance,
no longer
hurry
along country lanes,
no longer
remember
the mountain glowing
in a tangerine sunset,
no longer
recall
dancing in a colorless
Utah landscape
as I wave goodbye
to evening.

Jim Brosnan's publishing credits include Nameless Roads (Moon Pie Press, 2019), a 2019 Pushcart Prize nomination, and over 500 poems most recently in the Aurorean, Crossways (Ireland), Eunoia Review (Singapore), Nine Muses Poetry (Wales), Strand (India), Voices of the Poppies Anthology (UK) and Scarlet Leaf Review (Canada).

Baseball – Carson Pytell

It was as a child, after a little league game
In which I struck out twice and
Let up the winning run,
When my father told me that the
Baseball season is a stellar metaphor for life.
He didn't explain and I was too upset to ask,
But his voice dropped low when he said it
And he knelt to match my eyeline.

In a couple days, at our next game, I hit two doubles
And made a clutch catch to secure the win,
And as we were lining up to shake the other team's hands,
Seeing the defeat in their eyes and feeling
The victory in my chest, I caught on to what my father meant:
A golden sombrero today, a walk off tomorrow,
And time, however short, to reflect and reset
And prepare for the next game.

Carson Pytell is a poet and short fiction writer living in a very small town in upstate New York. His work has previously appeared or is forthcoming in such publications as Vita Brevis, Literary Yard, Leaves of Ink, Revolution John, Corvus Review, Gideon Poetry Review, Poetry Pacific, Futures Trading and Former People.

The Scribe and the Prophet - Greg Ramkawsky

You have read about the sunrise,
Colours of red and pink and gold
Shaded on the bellies of clouds,
Shining amber rays of light
Peaking above the iron hills:

"Earth has not anything to show more fair"

"Kissing with golden face the meadows green"

"Thy beams, so reverend and strong"

"An aimless smile that hovers in the air."

But have you awakened with the dawn,
Offered the sacrifice of eyes-wide-open,
Felt the soft warmth of bursting strand,
Observed the clamour of crimson battle,
Experienced the hope of dark deferred,
Or enjoyed the splendor of the King
Returning to the earth again?
Have you experienced the breaking light
Which causes you to live another day?

Greg Ramkawsky is a husband and father who also loves reading and writing, occasionally to his children's chagrin. A hopefully emerging poet, Greg has been published by Red Flag Poetry.

Incubator – Ali Grimshaw

And when you are hollowed
empty to the clean
that is when you know
the cycle complete

When you have sat with
all that was, and
all that could have been
held as one, in cupped palms

like a downy chick just released
fresh from the shell eager
beak cracking, forever free
light blinded and alive

to live outside.

Without breaking apart
how else will you learn
if flight is possible?

Ali Grimshaw is a hope rebel living in Portland, Oregon. Her poems have been published on Right Hand Pointing, Vita Brevis, Amethyst Review, and Ghost City Review.

Turning Point - Merril D. Smith

Winter, gloomy skies
and ghosts
that drift through dreams,
reminding us to remember
though we sleep to forget
as the snow piles higher and higher,
and what is the point of this story--
too grey and boring to be horror?
Then, a single yellow crocus blooms,
and a red-breasted robin trills to the sun--
then, at last, the page turns,
and a new chapter begins,
illustrated in blue, green, and gold.

Merril D. Smith is a historian and poet. Her poetry and stories have appeared recently in Rhythm & Bones, Vita Brevis, Streetlight Press, Ghost City, Twist in Time, Mojave Heart Review, Wellington Street Review, Blackbough Poetry, and Nightingale and Sparrow.

Little Moth Dancing - Joseph Marshall

And then out of the dark came a flutter of wings
Through an open window he came in search of light
Was it to be a sign or a metaphor
That in my darkest hour a moth came to dance?

So, as I sat there, arms folded, leaning forward
On a cold breath of wind, a moth came floating in
And proceeded to sway round the ceiling
As the man I knew lay in the room next door

And he was so still but asleep and dreaming
And as I watched from the end of the bed I thought
That there would be a chance, there was hope
I was just like the moth looking for the light

But life is cruel, takes what we love without mercy
And from the hospital room, my dad was taken
And then in the crematorium
We burnt his body, now he's only ashes

In the madness of it all, I'm left wondering
About what it is all for and what it really means
But I keep ending up recalling
How before that little moth came to dance

Little moth that came dancing
Were you there to mark the beginning of the end?
Moving as fluid as time
We don't have the hours for crying over mistakes

Little moth always in search
Of the brightest light, I'm thinking that we should be too.

Joseph Marshall is a 23-year-old amateur writer and aspiring novelist living in west Wales with his family and many pets. When he is not working on his first novella or cleaning holiday cottages, he is practicing his writing on his blog, The Inkfinger Entries, where he creates poetry for escapism and self-expression.

Thrive - Catherine Zickgraf

When the pain comes
like a fist through your ribs
to squeeze your soul in the hull
of its grip, lower shoulders, breathe.

When fight/flight kicks in
and hormones snake your neurons,
constrict your lungs, your heart works harder
and skin throbs, inhale through your spirit,
through your fingers. Find power
in breathing your own air.

Catherine Zickgraf's main jobs are to hang out with her family and write poetry. Her work has appeared in the Journal of the American Medical Association, Pank, Victorian Violet Press, and The Grief Diaries. Her recent chapbook, Soul Full of Eye, is published through Aldrich Press.

After Rejection - Theresa Burns

I sit in the back yard,
watch a wren build
a nest in the wren house.
The twig he lifts doesn't fit
through the small O
just right for his whirr-soft
body, so he drops it.
He lifts another & drops
it & then another.
All the while his wife
chatters like a fax machine
from within. One more
minute I stay & watch
before I step inside.
Enough to notice
that near-dead hydrangea,
in its fifth or sixth year,
finally reach past the switch-
grass for its sun.

Theresa Burns' poetry, reviews, and nonfiction have appeared in The New York Times, Prairie Schooner, Bellevue Literary Review, America Magazine, New Ohio Review, The Journal of the American Medical Association (JAMA), and elsewhere. She was nominated for a Pushcart Prize in 2018, and her chapbook of poems, Two Train Town, was recently published by Finishing Line Press. A long-time book editor in New York and Boston, she has taught writing at Seton Hall University, The Fashion Institute of Technology, and the 92nd Street Y.

Made in the USA
Middletown, DE
21 September 2020